Radical Christianity 101:
Empowering Your Disciples

By: Radical Launch

Unleashed Publishing, Inc.
975 Wayne Avenue #351
Chambersburg, Pa 17201

We can be reached by calling
(717) 860-1848 or through
our Website:
 unleashedpublishing.net

ISBN-13: 978-1-7333090-8-0
ISBN-10: 1-7333090-8-0

"I do not pray for these alone, but also for those who will believe in Me through their word; that they all may be one, as You, Father, are in Me, and I in You; that they also may be one in Us, that the world may believe that You sent Me. And the glory which You gave Me I have given them, that they may be one just as We are one: I in them, and You in Me; that they may be made perfect in one, and that the world may know that You have sent Me, and have loved them as You have loved Me." (Jesus praying in John 17:20-23)

Table of Contents

Making the Bible Relevant Today

Understanding Our Identity Through Jesus

In order to understand our identity, we need to understand the one who came to give us life and life everlasting. We cannot understand who we are unless we understand the One True Living God, Jesus Christ. In this section we are going to help you grasp a better understanding of the person, Jesus. What was His purpose and what did He really do for each of us? It is not enough to just know about Jesus; we need to build a relationship with Him. What does that look like in our lives? Let's learn how to see with the eyes of our hearts who the Bible says Jesus is and what His purpose was on earth.

Jesus talks about Eternal Life in John 17:1-5, giving us a better understanding of what He was doing while on earth:

"This is what Jesus prayed as he looked up into heaven, *"Father, the time has come. Unveil the glorious splendor of your Son so that I will magnify your glory! You have already given me authority over all people so that I may give the gift of eternal life to all those that you have given to me. Eternal Life means to know and experience Jesus Christ, as the Son Whom you have sent. I have glorified you on the earth by faithfully doing everything you've told me to do. So my Father, restore me back to the glory that we shared together when we were face-to-face before the universe was created."* (The Passion Translation)

Another translation tells us: *"After Jesus said this, He looked toward heaven and prayed: "Father, the hour has come. Glorify your Son, that your Son may glorify you. For you granted him authority over all people that he might give eternal life to all those you have given him. Now this is eternal life: that they know you, the only true God, and Jesus Christ, whom you have sent. I have brought you glory on earth by finishing the work you gave me to do. And now, Father, glorify me in your presence with the glory I had with you before the world began."* (NIV Translation)

Who Was Jesus?

John Chapter 17 shares the last prayer (recorded) that Jesus prayed and it was for you and I! That is how much He loved each one of us. He wanted us to know how much He loved us and that because He laid down His life to do the will of the Father, we get to join Him in unity with the Father. As humans, we struggle to grasp who Jesus really was. I pray that you will be able to understand the love and compassion of Jesus that gave Him the ability to lay down His life to die for you.

John Chapter 17 also tells us that Jesus gave the Father glory by faithfully fulfilling everything the Father asked Him to do. He fulfilled the call on His life and left a legacy that is still being increased through you today. If Jesus was asking the Father to restore Him back to the glory that they once shared, that indicates he took on a different role while on earth as Jesus. The purpose of Jesus in his life while on earth was to give the gift of eternal life and to take back the keys satan stole from Adam and Eve when he deceived them in the Garden of Eden. Jesus was here on earth to restore the relationship between us and God Almighty once again. Understanding how Jesus restored our relationship with Father God can only really be happen when we understand who Jesus was.

God had been looking for thousands of years for one who would redeem what man lost in the fall in the Garden of Eden. God could have done it all Himself, but God is all about relationship and He wants people to love Him as much as He loves them. God is not about control and He will not manipulate man into a relationship. As God considered many different men in the Bible, He found none who could redeem what Adam and Eve had lost. Isaiah 59 tells about the desperation of God as He searched for one to walk out a destiny of truly laying down their life to overcome the plans of the enemy, once and for all. God was looking for justice and was displeased that He found no one, not a single one, to intercede or intervene:

"He saw that there was no man, and wondered that there was no one to intercede; then his own arm brought him salvation, and his righteousness upheld him. He put on righteousness as a breastplate, and a helmet of salvation on his head; he put on garments of vengeance for clothing, and wrapped himself in zeal as a cloak. According to their deeds, so will he repay, wrath to his adversaries, repayment to his enemies; to the coastlands he will render repayment. So they shall fear the name of the LORD from the west, and his glory from the rising of the sun; for he will come like a rushing stream, which the wind of the LORD drives. And a Redeemer will come to Zion, to those in Jacob who turn from transgression, declares the LORD. And as for me, this is my covenant with them, says the LORD: My Spirit that is upon you, and my words that I have put in your mouth, shall not depart out of your mouth, or out of the mouth of your offspring, or out of the mouth of your children's offspring, says the LORD, from this time forth and forevermore."

Meditating on these scriptures should help you understand a little more of what God did for us through Jesus. God looked for someone to stand in righteousness and he found not one person. God was looking throughout the earth, looking for one who could stand and He found none. So He sent His own right arm. Looking up "right arm" in the Hebrew, *zĕrowa`* means arm or power, but going deeper into the Hebrew root word, Zara means to become pregnant or to be made pregnant; it could also be to sow a seed of justice or even to to take in the arms. I would like to propose that this is God speaking about the birth of Jesus who would be conceived by Mary. The seed of justice would be planted into the womb of Mary and it would bring forth a man who would walk in righteousness and be one who would deliver others by laying down His own life, being the "grain of wheat that must die to produce much fruit" which Jesus talks about in John 12:

"And Jesus answered them, "The hour has come for the Son of Man to be glorified. Truly, truly, I say to you, unless a grain of wheat falls into the earth and dies, it remains alone; but if it dies, it bears much fruit. Whoever loves his life loses it, and whoever hates his life in this world will keep it for eternal life. If anyone serves me, he must follow me; and where I am, there will my servant be also. If anyone serves me, the Father will honor him." (John 12:23- 26)

God sent His only begotten Son, Emmanuel, that He would look to the Father and know the Father's business. He put on the helmet of salvation (Hebrew word *yĕshuw`ah* meaning deliverance, salvation by God, victory) and the breastplate of righteousness (Hebrew word *tsĕdaqah* meaning righteousness of God's attribute or characteristic, or justice) on Him Who He sent. He put on the garment of vengeance which is the vengeance which Jehovah (God Almighty takes) by one man bearing the sins of ALL mankind. The Hebrew word for garment means to cover one's transgressions, deceit, or oppression. What if this means to clothe one person in the sin of the world? One man who knew no sin would take on our sin and die for us so that we could have eternal salvation and be delivered from our lifestyle of deathly sin to life everlasting? He wrapped Himself in zeal as a cloak (mantel or a priestly robe) is also an another reference to the love that He was wrapped in, the zeal of Jehovah, the ardent love which display strong enthusiasm or fervent devotion.

We need to understand more of what the scripture says about who Jesus would be. When God has two scriptures back to back stating the same thing, He is trying to get our attention. Something important is being revealed in Isaiah 7 where God gives us a prophetic description of who Jesus would be and when he was going to be born:

"Therefore the Lord himself will give you a sign. Behold, the virgin shall conceive and bear a son, and shall call his name Immanuel. He shall eat curds and honey when he knows how to refuse the evil and choose the good. For before the boy knows how to refuse the evil and choose the good, the land whose two kings you dread will be deserted."

Jesus would be born of a virgin and they would name him Emmanuel. The scripture says he would eat curds and honey when he knew how to refuse the evil and choose the good. Both scriptures say the same thing, helping us to understand Jesus also had to learn right from wrong and had to choose good and refuse evil. It was only once Jesus knew how to refuse evil and choose good that He would be given access to the authority that He would walk in while on earth. Scripture also tells us that Jesus grew in stature (maturity) and in favor (grace or that which affords Joy) with God and man (Luke 2:52).

Matthew Chapter 1 talks about Jesus being born to Mary, a virgin, conceived by the Holy Spirit. Jesus was not created through the marriage union of a man and a woman. Both the angels that visited Mary and Joseph told them Mary would give birth to a son who was conceived through the Holy Spirit and that His name would be Immanuel meaning "God with us". I believe that Jesus was fully man, born of a woman just like you and I. It was man (Adam and Eve) who lost their authority to satan when they ate of the tree of the knowledge of good and evil and it had to be a man to reclaim victory over satan. Isaiah 7 tells us that Immanuel (also known as

Jesus), who was born of a virgin (Mary) learned right from wrong and learned to refuse evil and choose good. We also need to learn right from wrong and to refuse evil and choose good. Jesus came to earth to be the way, to show us how to walk out our life and to go and do even greater because he first claimed victory for us on the cross. When God is talking about something very important in the Bible, He sometimes puts two scriptures back to back that talk about the same thing. God also shows us that Jesus was just a baby, born like you and I, and we also are born with a purpose that is far greater than we can imagine. Jesus also needed to learn right from wrong and to choose the good and refuse the evil. Isaiah 7 tells us that once He had learned these things, Jesus would eat curds and honey. The word curd in the Hebrew language (H2529) refers to a milk with an intoxicating power. Curds and Honey when joined together are delicacies provided by nature. According to this, God would pour out His power upon and through Jesus once He learned right from wrong.

Luke 2:52 says "... Jesus grew in wisdom and stature, and in favor with God and men." He walked out life on earth as a man for the first 31 years of His life, building character and learning from the Father, as well as man, while becoming who God created Him to be so that He could fulfill the call on His life. He fulfilled His purpose on Earth by walking in full obedience to His Father. Jesus was so in Love with His Father that He wanted to know where He was at all times. He was a Son who was undone by the Love of His Father.

In the Book of Daniel, God gives us some insight to the power that raised Jesus from the grave, the power that will rule and reign again on the earth. The power that will overcome all the evil of the enemy.

"As I looked, "thrones were set in place, and the Ancient of Days took his seat. His clothing was as white as snow; the hair of his head was white like wool. His throne was flaming with fire, and its wheels were all ablaze. A river of fire was flowing, coming out from before him. Thousands upon thousands attended him; ten thousand times ten thousand stood before him. The court was seated, and the books were opened. "Then I continued to watch because of the boastful words the horn was speaking. I kept looking until the beast was slain and its body destroyed and thrown into the blazing fire. (The other beasts had been stripped of their authority, but were allowed to live for a period of time.) "In my vision at night I looked, and there before me was one like a son of man, coming with the clouds of heaven. He approached the Ancient of Days and was led into his presence. He was given authority, glory and sovereign power; all nations and peoples of every language worshiped him. His dominion is an everlasting dominion that will not pass away, and his kingdom is one that will never be destroyed. (Daniel 7:9-14)

In the midst of Daniel's dream it talks about 10 horns and a boastful one that would rise up. In the discussion of the boastful horn, Daniel describes the overcoming power of Jesus. I believe this gives us an idea of what Jesus was going to accomplish as He laid down His own life to bear the sins of the world, to do the will of the Father, and to complete what He was called to accomplish, giving all glory to God. In this dream it describes the power and authority which would overthrow the enemy. The beast was slain and its body was destroyed and thrown into the blazing fire. Daniel saw the Ancient of Days (God Almighty) and Jesus was led into His presence where He was given authority, glory and sovereign power. His dominion would be an everlasting dominion that will not pass away and His kingdom would be one that will never be destroyed. Was this a dream of the day Jesus was resurrected? Know that the same power that raised Jesus from the dead also lives inside of you! After His resurrection, Jesus was given all authority, glory, and sovereign power. His dominion will be everlasting and will not pass away and His kingdom will be one that will never be destroyed.

Wow, that is powerful! Jesus laying down his life to gain everlasting life not just for himself, but for each of us. He was born as a man of a woman to claim back the keys of authority that were stolen by satan when Adam and Eve were deceived in the Garden. As Jesus was baptized, the Holy Spirit descended upon Him in bodily form like a dove for all to see which is described very clearly in Luke 3:21-22:

"Now when all the people were baptized, it came to pass, that Jesus also being baptized, and praying, the heaven was opened, And the Holy Ghost descended in a bodily shape like a dove upon him, and a voice came from

heaven, which said, Thou art my beloved Son; in thee I am well pleased."

In that moment as the Holy Spirit descended upon Jesus, God almighty rested on Jesus in bodily form. What if in that moment, God almighty found a man worthy to carry His spirit?

In those next moments after Jesus was baptized, the Spirit led Him into the wilderness for 40 days where He was tempted by the devil. During this time, He fasted for 40 days and 40 nights (Luke 4). As you meditate on these scriptures, you will see how satan tempted Jesus. In these scriptures God has placed many nuggets of information we can receive to help us walk out our journey with Jesus. After Jesus had ended His fast, the devil tried to question His identity while also tempting Him by saying: "If you are the Son of God, tell this stone to become bread." (Luke 4:3). Jesus' response is key: "man shall not live on bread alone". Jesus tells His disciples later that His food is to do the will of the Father and that he eats meat that the disciples do not know about. "My food", said Jesus, "is to do the will of him who sent me and to finish his work." (John 4:34 NIV) The King James Version of the Bible actually records it this way: "I have meat to eat that ye know not of … My meat is to do the will of Him that sent me, and to finish His work." (John 4:32-34)

It is important to note that Jesus was being tempted by the devil, not by God. "When tempted, no one should say, 'God is tempting me.' For God cannot be tempted by evil, nor does He tempt anyone; but each person is tempted when they are dragged away by their own evil desire and enticed. Then, after desire has conceived, it gives birth to sin; and sin, when it is full-grown, gives birth to death." (James 1:13) The devil knew the power and authority that Jesus had inside of Him. The enemy has many tactics to get us to take our focus off of God and turn our attention to himself. The enemy attacked again at the end of those 40 days of fasting when Jesus was hungry. He literally took Jesus to a high place and showed Him all the kingdoms of the world and said: "I will give you all their authority and splendor; it has been given to me, and I can give it to anyone I want to. If you worship me, it will all be yours." Jesus wisely answered, "it is written: 'Worship the Lord your God and serve him only'." (Luke 4:6) The devil was not done tempting Jesus though, and this time the devil took Him to highest point of the temple in Jerusalem to try to tempt Jesus by challenging Him to throw himself down from the highest part of the temple if He really was the Son of God, saying: "He will command his angels concerning you to guard you carefully; they will lift you up in their hands, so that you will not strike your foot against a stone." (Luke 4:10) Jesus replied, "Do not put the Lord your God to the test." Jesus knew scripture and was not confused or distracted by the tactics of the enemy. God says get the scripture in you and let it become you. The Bible tells us to meditate day and night on The Word. Know the truth and the truth will set you free; the truth did set Jesus free and the enemy didn't succeed in provoking Jesus or tempting Him.

Jesus talked about the power and authority that he has given us: *"I saw Satan fall like lightning from heaven. I have given you authority to trample on snakes and scorpions and to overcome all the power of the enemy; nothing will harm you. However, do not rejoice that the spirits submit to you, but rejoice that your names are written in heaven."* (Luke 10:18-20) Jesus sent out the 70 before Him. Jesus sent them out two by two to go into all the places where He was about to go. He sent them out to heal the sick and to tell people that the Kingdom of God was near. He sent them out as "lambs among the wolves". Jesus told them that the harvest was ready but that the workers were few". He was giving them everything they needed to bring in the "harvest as they went. They were very excited as they returned because they saw demons submit to them in Jesus' name. Jesus replied that He had seen satan fall like lightning from heaven. He reminded them that He had already given them authority and power. He also told them to not spend their time rejoicing over the enemy submitting to them, but to celebrate that their names were written in heaven. He wanted them to be heavenly focused.

Because of Who Jesus was and because of what He overcame, we get to walk in His Power and Authority to destroy the plans of the enemy in our own sphere of influence. Take your authority in Christ and allow the Power of the Holy Spirit to rule and reign in and throughout your life as you allow the Father to embrace you in a deep relationship that will fill you to overflowing with abundant love, peace, and joy. That relationship will give you hope, because Hope has a name and His name is Jesus! Each one of us is called to something different, but in everything we do, we are to go into the world proclaiming the gospel in the way that God has gifted each of us. When we look for where the Father is and hear His voice and allow Jesus inside of us to rise up while being led by the Holy Spirit, we will know who God is highlighting for us to have a divine appointment with. It is not about preaching to everyone you see, look to where the Father has already prepared the soil of someone's heart, and focus your efforts there; Look where the Holy Spirit knows He has prepared their hearts to receive the Good News.

Understanding the Ministry of Jesus

How did Jesus minister? The focus of the ministry of Jesus was empowering others. Scripture says He only did what the Father showed Him and He only spoke what the Father said. Let's see what that looked like through the times when some of the disciples were asked to join Jesus and come and follow Him in the Gospels.

Jesus Empowered His Disciples

As Jesus was leaving Galilee one day, He approached Philip who was from the town of Bethsaida. When Jesus approached him, He said to Philip "come follow me." Philip went and found Nathanael to share the news that they had found the one Moses had written about. Nathanael did not believe the news. Nathanael still went with Philip in spite of his disbelief. Jesus was about to change his entire life in a moment. As Nathanael approached, Jesus called out the greatness in Nathanael by saying, "Here is a true Israelite, in whom there is nothing false." (John 1:43-51) Nathanael must have been stunned in that moment. Jesus than shared that He had seen Nathanael sitting under the fig tree when Philip called him. Jesus was not there with Philip so this got Nathanael's attention! How do you think Jesus knew this? He had to know that information from Father God, because he did not see it in the natural. Jesus tapped into the prophetic to know where Nathanael was located and He could only do that through the relationship He had with Father God. God showed Him Nathanael, and God also spoke through Jesus the words to capture the heart of Nathanael. When Nathanael heard Jesus tell him where he just was, those very words opened up an understanding of the supernatural realm of Heaven, giving Nathanael the understanding that Jesus was the Son of God. Jesus also spoke these words to Nathanael: "You believe because I told you I saw you under the fig tree. You shall see greater things than that... I tell you the truth, you shall see heaven open, and the angels of God ascending and descending on the Son of Man." (John 1:50-51)

God moved through Jesus to call Nathanael forth to be one of the amazing disciples of Jesus. Jesus moved in the prophetic and was so full of the love of the Father that the heavens opened up over Him to allow Nathanael to see who He really was. He was the Truth and the Truth set Nathanael free from his unbelief and set him on a path and a journey to see even greater things.

The Transformation of Zacchaeus

What about Zacchaeus (Luke 19:2-9)? What did it look like when Jesus ministered to Zacchaeus?

Zacchaeus was a Tax Collector. He was apparently a short man whom we don't know a lot about. What we can see in scripture is that this man had heard about a man named Jesus and he wanted to at least see who He was. When we take the time to talk with God as we read the scriptures, we can see the scriptures unfold before our eyes and we can learn from this story in our lives today.

Zacchaeus was a short man who most likely struggled all of his life with being teased. In our own lives we can see people like that who get pushed aside all the time until they start to feel unworthy and sometimes rise up with an angry spirit that is not Godly. What if Zacchaeus was smart, but because of being short no one ever saw his greatness? I believe to that be a Tax Collector you would need to have some intelligence and education. The Bible tells us Zacchaeus was thought of as a sinner by the rest of the people in the area. He was also known to be rich in an area where most people didn't have wealth. He was doing well in his career and was in a position over others in order to be the Chief Tax Collector. He was most likely very knowledgeable and knew how to get the money people owed in taxes. A person like this probably hurt a lot of people along the way, right or wrong. No matter who this man was, apparently he was hungry for something more in his life. He was hungry to know Jesus. He wanted to meet Him or to at least lock eyes on

Him as He walked down the street. Zacchaeus had a passion to overcome every obstacle in his way to see who this Jesus was. He was willing to go out on a tree limb to get up above everyone else to be in a better position to see.

As Zacchaeus climbed up that tree, I believe that his hunger pulled on heaven. In that moment, I believe God saw the hunger in Zacchaeus. I believe heaven and earth met in that moment and time stood still just for one man who the world did not value. God saw this amazing son who was hungry for something more in his life and He highlighted him for Jesus. We can look at our own lives and see moments like this where heaven moved and earth stood still for us until the Lord fully encountered us in an answer to our hunger.

What are you hungry for in life? Will your hunger cause heaven to come into your life to change the very atmosphere where you stand?

I believe Father God highlighted Zacchaeus to Jesus, showing the importance of our relationship with God the Father. In the moment when Jesus locked eyes on Zacchaeus, I believe the Father revealed to Jesus who Zacchaeus was. When Jesus saw Zacchaeus, time stopped and the direction Jesus was heading in was shifted and directed towards just one man.

Can you imagine being that person and what it might have felt like to walk in his shoes all of his life? Can you imagine being Zacchaeus in that tree, locking eyes on Jesus after going out on the limb of life to know who

Jesus really was? My heart races just thinking of that moment! Can you imagine that moment when Jesus' path changed and He headed towards Zacchaeus in that tree? What grabs my attention is that Jesus knew Zacchaeus' name and wanted to go to his house to eat.

Can you imagine Jesus as a man, standing before you and wanting to go to your house to eat with you? In that moment, Jesus shut the mouth of the enemy, silencing his accusations and also shut the mouths of all those who were muttering about who Zacchaeus was. In that moment, Jesus also became the door that opened the heart of the Father to embrace Zacchaeus for the first time in his life. Jesus is the only way to the Father. I believe that through His relationship with the Father, Jesus knew who was pulling on the heart strings of the Father. I believe Jesus used the prophetic to truly know who Zacchaeus was and chose to speak life into him. I believe Jesus had access to the compassionate heart of the Father and that allowed Him to unlock the pain in Zacchaeus. I believe in that moment, a lifetime of pain left Zacchaeus and God the Father touched His son, Zacchaeus, for the first time. In that one moment, Jesus saw a sinner who was hated by people turn into a man full of love. It takes a lot of love to be willing to give half of everything you own to the poor and to also give back 4 times the amount of money to anyone you wronged.

What a transformation! It truly was an encounter with the one true living God, Jesus Christ. We also have those opportunities when we have a relationship with Jesus,

God the Father, and the Holy Spirit and we can also see the "Zacchaeus" in our life transformed in a heart beat.

Jesus Empowered the Woman at the Well

John Chapter 4 talks about an encounter Jesus had with the woman at the well.   I would like to look at the scripture to see how Jesus ministered to her. This moment in time didn't just impact one person, it impacted an entire town through one woman having her moment with Jesus. The impact Jesus has on our lives should also impact more than just ourselves; our encounters with Jesus should also impact everyone we encounter in our lives afterwards.

According to the scripture, Jesus was tired from His journey and sat down by a well at about noon that day. Jesus needed to find rest and in that place, the Father brought a woman to Jesus who was in need of a life-changing encounter. This was currently a Samaritan well, but it also belonged to the ancestors of Jacob who was a Jew. In those days, It was not lawful for a Jew to interact with a Samaritan, so why did Jesus go to that particular well? I believe the Father led Him to a divine appointment with a woman on her own journey, a woman who needed to find hope in her life or maybe she was just looking be loved for who she was.

This moment in time was so impactful that it changed the culture and made salvation available to not only the the Jewish people, but also to the Samaritans. Jesus watched where the Father was and went where the Father was highlighting for him to go for his next divine appointment. He stepped away from His disciples and followed His Father. He must have done this before, because the disciples just continued on their journey without complaint. The Father has His heart set on reconciliation with His people and He was about to reconcile His daughter's heart back to Him; the Father was about to reconcile an entire generation of Samaritans back to Himself.

The woman at the well told Jesus that it was her ancestor Jacob's well. She was a descendant of Jacob, yet not considered a Jew. In God's eyes this didn't matter. In this story of the woman at the well, she was a woman by herself at the well in the heat of the middle of the day collecting water for her family. What does that say about her? That she had no friends? No one to join her on her journey? Was she an outcast who was unwanted? How many of us have been in this position at some point of our lives? Have you ever found yourself with no one to walk beside you, feeling lonely, unloved and unwanted? The Father saw her and had compassion for her and drew Jesus away from the disciples to meet with this one woman alone.

When the Samaritan Women came to draw water, Jesus was right there waiting for her along with the Father. Jesus is right there waiting for us also in our time of need. The Samaritan women represents someone who in their culture would have been unworthy to speak to or maybe even considered to be an outcast. Jesus didn't bow to culture; He followed His Father in Heaven, bringing Heaven to Earth. It was not acceptable for a Jewish man to approach a Samaritan woman either, but Jesus stepped across cultural limitations to allow a woman to encounter her Heavenly Father for the first time in her life. The disciples had gone on to town to buy food yet Jesus was about to eat from the Tree of Life.

Jesus asked this woman to give Him a drink from the well. I believe she was stunned by Him asking because it was unlawful for a Jew to lower themselves by speaking to a Samaritan. Jesus' ministry serves as an example of how to walk out our own lifestyle of Christianity. He knew what the Father wanted to talk with her about and spoke to her in a way that was inviting, saying: *"If you knew the gift of God and who it is that asks you for a drink, you would have asked him and he would have given you living water."* He speaks to her in a way that causes a question in her heart: What is this living water He talks about? Who is this man? Can you imagine being that woman with Jesus sitting there asking you the same question?

I believe His eyes pierced her soul and pushed away the darkness as He spoke life into her. He spoke in a way which provoked questions. This woman was so impacted by her encounter with Jesus that her whole world changed in a moment; in a heartbeat she was forever impacted. Jesus told the woman, "believe in me" (John 4). Jesus then shared with the woman that a time would come (and it is now) that the worshipers would worship in spirit and truth and that they would worship neither on "this mountain nor Jerusalem". He was speaking about how as we receive Jesus into our hearts, we will worship the Lord in Spirit and in truth. It is not a place, but within us where He now will reside once we accept Jesus into our hearts. We cannot get Jesus from anyone else or go to a specific place to receive Jesus. As we worship Him with all of our heart, soul, spirit, and mind, we are looking to Him as our Lord and not looking to another person to be our higher power or to be His translator for us. He alone is your living water. He alone is your salvation. In him, you will thirst no more.

The woman at the well was transformed by her encounter with Jesus. She was a new person, transformed and on a journey that would lead an entire town to Christ. This woman came to the well with a heavy heart and left with a new found life of purpose. Jesus ministered to her using the prophetic, using love, and using compassion. He never used His prophetic gifts to judge her or destroy her, but instead He chose to give her life. Our words to other people need to give life and not death. Our words should empower others and not devalue them. This woman was so impacted by Jesus that she left her water jar behind and went back to a village that most likely hated her, filled to overflowing with a love that she poured out into each one of them while telling them what she just encountered and saying: "Could this be the Messiah?" This woman who walked in the hottest time of the day to get water by herself most likely would admit she had no friends, but the impact she made on that same town as she shared the Testimony of Jesus convinced them to drop everything they were doing to come check out this Jesus. Do you allow the Jesus inside of you to impact others in that same way? What if we would allow Jesus to rise up inside of us to touch the community where we live?

The disciples came back and had no ability to understand what Jesus had been doing while they had gone to get food. They were concerned for Him, thinking He needed food, however, Jesus had been fed spiritually through His encounter with the Samaritan woman. He told the disciples, "I have food to eat that you know nothing about." … "My food, "said Jesus, "is to do the will of Him who sent me and to finish His work." Are we looking to see where the Father is highlighting for us to go next? Are you experiencing Jesus rising up inside of you everyday to minister to the one in front of you? When people walk away from you, can they say they feel empowered or discouraged? Jesus' way of ministry looked different than the way we walk out ministry today and we need to take a step back and look at how Jesus ministered and apply that today in our lives.

Understanding the Purpose of Jesus

Jesus had a purpose on this earth, just like each one of us. Through a relationship with Jesus, you will have a greater ability to understand your purpose in life. Jesus went to the cross to die for our sins and through His death, we have access to eternal life through salvation. Romans 6:6 speaks of how our old self was crucified with Christ on the cross so "that the body of sin would be done away with that we should no longer be slaves to sin."

At the Wedding at Cana, Mary asked Jesus to help when the master of ceremonies was in need of more wine. Jesus said to his mother that his time had not come yet. Mary told the servants to do what Jesus said. This became the first miracle recorded in the Bible. Jesus told the servants to fill the stone water purification jars with water to the brim. Jesus didn't touch the water pots nor the water. However, God used the servants to bring forth a miracle, maybe the first miracle attributed to Jesus. If you relate this story to our lives and consider that when we accept Jesus as our Lord and Savior, we become the stone pots filled to overflowing with the Holy Spirit pouring out the new wine of Jesus. We become vessels of God, overflowing with the Holy Spirit to pour out Jesus into the lives of those God puts in front of us. When completely surrendering our lives (as in John 17), we also can walk out a life unto the Lord, giving Jesus the glory as He lives through our lives like Peter, John, Paul, James, Phillip,

Stephen, and so many other true followers of Jesus did. Even though they were not necessarily known in the world, I believe they are known in Heaven.

As we learn to allow the love of Jesus to wash over us filling us with His abundant joy, we will start to love ourselves as the Father loves us so that we can also love Him the way He loves us. In that place of love, we will also have the ability to love our neighbors as we love ourselves. We are a vessel that will carry Jesus everywhere we go, taking the light of Christ into all the world and displacing the darkness while revealing the truth of Jesus by using the gifts that Jesus also used to reach out to all: the gifts of the prophetic, healing, raising the dead and setting the captives free.

As you fully surrender your life to Jesus, you will be a witness unto all the world starting right where you are by loving the hell out of people, seeing them set free, seeing them healed, and seeing them on fire for God. Jesus fully surrendered His life to do the will of the Father. He went to the cross as a man without sin to take on the sin of the world to overcome the plans of the enemy and to take back the keys which the devil took from Adam and Eve in the Garden of Eden. In his resurrection, Jesus overcame the plans of the enemy and gave each of us everlasting life. He died so we don't have to die. It is a free gift to all. You could never be good enough to earn it; it is a gift given to each who believes in Jesus through the grace of Father God.

As we are embraced by the one who loved us from the beginning of time (Jesus), we are able to love others through the love of the Father. We get to love people to life while seeing the Jesus in you become more and more evident as we re-present Jesus to others through our transformed lives.

Jesus set an example for us as He ministered to others here on earth to show each of us how to minister to others. When He completed what He was called to complete in order that we could have eternal salvation through believing and receiving Him into our lives, He came back to live within each of us. He brings us the same power and authority He was given to do the will of the Father so that we can walk out our surrendered lives for Him, giving Him glory.

Let's take a journey to see what it was like for Peter and John when they saw their first miracle. Let's see how they ministered as they revealed Jesus to the crippled man at the Gate called Beautiful. Peter and John were heading to the Temple like they had many other times. They had already experienced the day of Pentecost when the power of God came upon them and they experienced the Baptism of Holy Spirit. It seemed this day was no different than so many other days in their lives, or was it the beginning of a completely new season of their lives? As Peter and John walked up to the gate called Beautiful, they saw the crippled man who had been placed there by others, they had seen him on many other days as they headed into the temple. According to the scripture, this man was crippled since birth and he was placed at this gate every day to beg. Peter and John would have walked past this man many other times, but this time was different, this time the crippled man captured their attention. This man had been begging for years in this same place, but his life was about to change. Peter and John looked straight into the crippled man's eyes and instructed him by saying: "Look at us". The crippled man looked at the two expecting to receive alms. He was expecting a monetary gift but this time the gift was in a different form. Peter spoke to the man, saying "Silver and Gold I do not have, but what I have I give you. In the name of Jesus Christ of Nazareth, walk." Peter then reached down and grabbed the man to pull him to his feet.

As we learn to allow the love of Jesus to wash over us, filling us with His abundant Love, we will start to love ourselves as the Father loves us so that we can then love Him the same way He loves us. With that love we will also have the ability to love our neighbor as we love ourselves. We are a vessel that will carry Jesus everywhere we go, taking the light of Christ into all the world and displacing the darkness while also revealing the truth of Jesus. This will give us the ability to reach out to all people we meet through the prophetic, healing, raising the dead, casting out demons, and setting the captives free. As you fully surrender your life to Jesus, you will be a witness unto all the world, starting right where you are by loving the "hell" out of people and seeing people set free, healed, and on fire for God. It is not about converting people to our particular denomination as much as it is about loving people to life and letting others see the Jesus in you as you re-present Jesus to others through your life.

As the ministry of Jesus intensified, the religious leaders of those days became more and more concerned for their own positions. They became more and more provoked by the darkness in their own hearts and started to do whatever they could to trap Him and discredit Him. Finally, at the Festival of Dedication in Jerusalem when Jesus was in the temple courts walking in Solomon's Colonnade, the Jews who were there gathered around him, saying, *"How long will you keep us in suspense? If you are the Messiah, tell us plainly."* Jesus answered, *"I did tell you, but you do not believe. The works I do in my Father's name testify about me, but you do not believe because you are not my sheep. My sheep listen to my voice; I know them, and they follow me. I give them eternal life, and they shall never perish; no one will snatch them out of my hand. My Father, who has given them to me, is greater than all; no one can snatch them out of my Father's hand. I and the Father are one."* (John 10:22-30). Even though they were the ones who had asked Jesus if He was the Messiah, when He answered they refused to believe Him and instead chose to stone Him as they were convinced that His claim was blasphemy.   The awesome thing is that this is the same location of the first miracle which was accomplished through Peter and John in Acts 3. Jesus chose to reveal through Peter and John the first tangible fruit of the Messiah. The ministry of The Anointed One continued through these two uneducated, ordinary men who "spent time with Jesus" performing their first healing miracle in the same exact physical location where Jesus was asked if He was actually the Messiah. The same Jesus that lived in and through Peter and John, giving them the courage and confidence to be vessels that carried Jesus in a way where their message touched the world with signs and wonders, lives inside of you also when you believe in Jesus Christ. Go into all the world proclaiming your message as Jesus tells the disciples that His prayer in John 17:20 is not just for them, but "for all those who would believe in Him through their message". We all have a message and it is only by sharing the Testimony of Jesus in our lives that we shall overcome the darkness in our world and actually undo the works of the devil.

The purpose of Jesus was to bring to us our ability to come into wholeness with God once again where the Holy Spirit will reside in us and move through us to reveal Jesus inside of us to those around us. Your message is unique to you and will reveal Jesus to all those whom God places in front of you. Jesus completed what He was called to complete as He lay His life down so that we would have life and life more abundant while in the land of the living as well as eternal life. Jesus gave us the same glory the Father gave him. Jesus actually receives glory through our surrendered lives. Go and "leak" Jesus to the World. Go and embrace others with the love of the Father. Be led by the Holy Spirit wherever you go. Fully surrender your life to Jesus and become one with Jesus as He is one with the Father and allow the Holy Spirit to lead you into all the ways of God one moment at a time and one person at a time.

"My prayer is not for them alone. I pray also for those who will believe in me through their message, that all of them

38

may be one, Father, just as you are in me and I am in you. May they also be in us so that the world may believe that you have sent me. I have given them the glory that you gave me, that they may be one as we are one— I in them and you in me—so that they may be brought to complete unity. Then the world will know that you have sent me and have loved them even as you have loved me. Father, I want those you have given me to be with me where I am, and to see my glory, the glory you have given me because you loved me before the creation of the world." (John 17:20-24)

As we walk out our lives, fully embracing Jesus, we need to stay continually filled with the Holy Spirit.

Understanding the Power and Authority of Jesus

Jesus Fulfilled His Purpose So We Would Have the Greater

Jesus gave His disciples the authority to heal the sick, to cast out demons, to set the captives free, to bind up the broken hearted, and to raise the dead. After Jesus was resurrected, He spent time with the disciples teaching them and sharing many things with them. Jesus told them as He departed from them that the comforter would come to dwell with them. He told that He had to go, so that the greater would come. Through the Holy Spirit, we become the very Temple of God - a mighty vessel carrying His presence. Before Jesus departed from the disciples, he told them to go and wait for the promise of the Father. He continued on to remind them that while John had baptized with water, they would be baptized with the Holy Spirit (Acts 1) to receive power. As they spent time in prayer in the Upper Room, the Holy Spirit came upon them on the Day of Pentecost. The Baptism of the Holy Spirit empowers us with inner strength through His Spirit. Paul refers to this inner strength in Ephesians 3:16 telling us: *"I pray that from His glorious, unlimited resources He will empower you with inner strength through His Spirit."*

Jesus told His disciples He needed *"to leave so that the Comforter would be able to come to abide in you forever"*. (John 14:16) Jesus breathed on them so they would receive the Holy Ghost. *"Then said Jesus to them again,*

Peace be unto you: as my Father hath sent me, even so send I you. And when he had said this, he breathed on them, and saith unto them, Receive ye the Holy Ghost". (John 20:21-22) They already believed in Jesus and had walked with Him for over three years. It was not about just repeating a prayer for them to be instantly overcome by the Spirit of God. I believe there is no one set way in which each of us receives the Holy Spirit. Throughout the entire Book of Acts, there are many instances where people received the Baptism of the Holy Spirit before Water Baptism. There are also times it happened after Water Baptism and there are times when it all happened at the same time. I believe that it happened for Paul during the encounter when he was knocked off his horse and encountered Jesus. The Bible also tells of an entire group of Gentiles starting to speak in tongues as the Holy Spirit fell upon their group while Peter was speaking to them about the free gift of Jesus. He proclaimed that anyone who believed would receive forgiveness of sins through the name of Jesus and the entire group began speaking in tongues (Acts 10: 44-48). Peter then asked if anyone could forbid or refuse water for Baptizing these people, seeing that they had already received the Holy Spirit just as the disciples had. This tells us of an incredible encounter where the Holy Spirit crashed in on an entire group and it was not about praying a prayer; It was through a heart connect with God. The Baptism of the Holy Spirit was not just reserved for a select group of people. Philip was called by the Angel of the Lord to go to the desert road to meet the Ethiopian eunuch (Acts 8:26-39). Philip followed to the Lord's instructions and went over to the chariot and heard the Ethiopian eunuch reading in the Book of Isaiah. Through this divine encounter, the eunuch was able to learn more from Philip about what he was reading in Isaiah. It also opened the door for Philip to speak to him about Jesus. As they went past some water, the Ethiopian eunuch asked if he could be baptized and Philip baptized him and the Spirit of the Lord then took Philip away and the eunuch went on his way, rejoicing. Clearly the Ethiopian eunuch was transformed by this encounter and after his baptism experienced the full measure of the Joy that only comes from an encounter with Jesus. Acts 3:19 talks about repentance as an actual turn around which allows us to return to God. Upon repentance, God will erase your sins and a time of refreshing will come through the presence of the Lord. I believe you will see a complete change in a person when they accept Jesus as their Lord and Savior.

Later on in Acts, Paul came upon 12 disciples in Ephesus and asked them a question that baffled me when I first read it. Paul asked them, "Did you receive the Holy Spirit when you believed?" (Acts 19:2-7) These disciples replied that they had not even heard there was a Holy Spirit! Wow! I was undone! Paul asked this approximately 10-15 years after Jesus was crucified. These were disciples! I could understand this if they were just regular people who have not been reached yet, but they were disciples! They had been baptized in the Baptism of Repentance of John. When Paul laid hands on them, they were Baptized in the Holy Spirit and something extraordinary happened: The Holy Spirit came upon them and they spoke in tongues and prophesied! I believe this points to the importance of receiving the Holy Spirit in order to be able to effectively communicate with the Lord. The Gift of Tongues is a private prayer language through which we can trust the Holy Spirit to help us to pray when we have run out of words and when we do not even know what or how to pray. The Gift of Prophesy allows us to hear what the Lord is sharing with us in order to build up the Body of Christ. What if the Church had already started to shift outside the heart of God just a short 10-15 years after Jesus was crucified? Yes, they still could have been doing good things, but how much can we as humans "do" for God? When we truly receive the Baptism of the Holy Spirit, there is a transformation in our lives. The importance of seeing Christ rise up inside of us comes when we live a fully surrendered life. It is only by laying down our lives and choosing to surrender to Him and His leading that can effectively overcome the world and bring His kingdom to earth as it is in heaven. Jesus gets glory through our surrendered lives just as Father God got glory when Jesus surrendered His life and laid it down for all of mankind to be redeemed on the Cross.

Applying the Bible to Your Life

Becoming Christian Disciples

Jesus overcame the broken systems of this world which are not in alignment with the kingdom of God, systems which are designed to keep men trapped where they are in all sorts of bondage and slavery where they are not able to live but are merely surviving. As Christians who have chosen to invite Jesus into our hearts and to be led by the Holy Spirit during our daily walk of Christianity, we have access to life and life more abundant (John 10:10). Because Jesus overcame the world we are able to overcome the world and all it brings by choosing to transform our minds by reading the very word of God so that it will penetrate deeply into our hearts and we will come alive and bit by bit we will surrender every single aspect of our lives to God so that He can help us to reflect Jesus more thoroughly each day.

The parable of the wheat and the tares illustrates the fact that the world has sown some seeds within our hearts that are not of God's kingdom, yet God leaves them there until it is time for the full Harvest to be collected. I believe that this points to an ever-increasing need for us to pursue healing and heart wholeness with our Heavenly Father. When I consider the parable of the wheat and the tares, things become a little bit more clear to me. God loves us so much that He doesn't want to pull out the tares/weeds that satan has sown in our hearts because that would risk uprooting the new Fruit of the Spirit which Father God knows is growing now that we have let His Son become our Master Gardener, the one who tends to the Garden that is in our hearts. God knows that eventually the Holy Spirit will reveal to us exactly what it is that we need to set us free from worldly snares so that we can become who it is He made us to be! Consider Heaven's Standard and be set apart for His use as you allow Him to transform you from Glory (where you opened your heart to Him) to Glory (where you actually reflect Him well).

Once we become transformed by washing our minds with the Word of God (Ephesians 5:26), we are then able to begin to focus on helping other people learn who it is that He says they are so that they too may start to live life more abundant in Jesus (John 10:10). One of the greatest things that the Body of Christ needs to begin to do effectively today is to choose to truly disciple others. We need to train and equip others so that they can overcome the obstacles in their lives and become who Father God made them to be so that they can step into their proper positions within the Body of Christ and the Body of Christ can then move forward together in unity, following Jesus Christ who is the head (Colossians 1:18)!

Our biggest challenge may be developing a way to remove ourselves from the influences of the culture within which we are living in order to train and teach people in a Biblical fashion. We need to seek God's heart on strategic teaching within the Kingdom and then implement that as we disciple others. Jesus showed an incredibly courageous model when He was teaching the disciples. In a revolutionary approach, Jesus simply told the disciples that they had been given all they needed to cast out demons and heal the sick - He told them to go and do it! Don't even take a change of clothes! Just go and do it and if you're not welcomed somewhere, don't get offended, just take your peace with you and knock the dust off your feet (Matthew 10:14) and know that it's going to be okay.

Within today's Church, we struggle with this simple approach. We've developed huge lists of requirements that people have to meet before they're even allowed to participate and work within their area of gifting. We also have huge, huge requirements for people who have backslidden, in order to make sure that they are properly reinstated within our predetermined Christian hierarchy. We have all these manmade requirements which, quite frankly, I don't see within the pages of the Bible. I definitely don't see them reflected when I look to Jesus as my example of how to be a "Leader" within the Kingdom. So, the question is: are we creating Milestones that people need to actually accomplish within their Christian walk in order to be recognized in certain positions? Or are we actually creating Millstones for ourselves?

All of these requirements and positions seem to be manmade to me. I am not convinced that they will stand the test of time and endure the fire of God on that day when He burns up all the stubble (1 Corinthians 3:13). I believe that as the Church, and as representatives of the Kingdom of God, we can do better. I believe that there's a way to train people and equip them and teach them in a loving manner that honors who it is that God made them to be right from day one. I believe that when somebody is baptized with the Holy Spirit, they have the full Holy Spirit - there is no Junior Holy Spirit. I believe that what Jesus accomplished on the Cross most assuredly is good enough for each and every one of us to enter in to our relationship with Him.

When we choose to invite Jesus in to our hearts to be our Lord and Savior, ALL of Heaven celebrates (Luke 15:7)!!! Heaven celebrates the unfolding of Father God's Plan - the Plan He birthed before the foundation of the world (Ephesians 1:4)! He is the beginning and the end (Revelation 22:13) of His Plan! From the very beginning it was about choice - do you choose life through obedience or do you choose to pursue personal knowledge by entering into rebellion? We were in Him before He spoke the Universe into existence (Ephesians 1:4) and lovingly made Adam and Eve. He knows everything and He has had a glorious Plan all along! For He is the author and finisher of our faith (Hebrews 12:2) and when we choose to place our trust in Him through faith, we have chosen to become a part of His Plan. When we choose to follow Jesus and allow ourselves to be transformed by the renewing of our minds (Romans 12:2), we have chosen to become partners with Heaven, allowing His Plan to unfold within our lives.

Closing the Doors of our Past

Jesus tells us in the Bible that we are either for Him or against Him (Matthew 12:30). Jesus urges us to "follow me"! The Bible also tells us in Psalms 24:7 to "lift up you gates" to let the "King of Glory" come in. The Bible reassures us that the "gates of hell" will not prevail against us (Matthew 16:18). We are gateways, designed to release either heaven or hell depending upon whom we are serving. Before we come to know Jesus, the Lord of Glory, and make Him the Lord of our lives, we are serving the lord of darkness, satan, who rules this fallen world whether we are aware of it or not.

The Four Doors of Legal Attack

Jesus overcame the world that we also could be overcomers. Jesus overcame death that we might have life and life more abundant (John 10:10). Once we invite Jesus into our hearts we have begun to overcome the world. Jesus tells us that although we are "in the world, we are no longer of the world" (John 15:9).
However, while we were in the world we may have opened ourselves to continuing attack by satan, the enemy of our souls. There are four "doors" which we can open that give the enemy access to our lives; these doors are fear, anger, sexual promiscuity, and any participation in occult activities.

When we act in fear it is because we are not trusting in God. The Bible tells us that "He did not give us a spirit of fear" (2 Timothy 1:7) but He gave us boldness and confidence and a spirit of might and a sound mind. The Bible also tells us that perfect 48 love casts out all fear (1 John 4:18).

Anger and acting in anger is clearly not of God because Jesus tells us that if we are even angry with someone it is as if we have murdered them (Matthew 5:21-22). When we act in anger that is clearly us choosing (whether we know it or not) to partner with satan and his ways, also known as the ways of the world. The Bible tells us that satan is the ruler of this world (Ephesians 2:2 and John 12:31) even though he actually lost all authority when Jesus went to the Cross and then descended to hell and took the keys from satan and then ascended to heaven to sit at the right hand of the Father who gave Jesus ALL Authority on earth and in Heaven (Matthew 28:18).

The next-door of legal access for satan within our lives can be opened through acts of sexual promiscuity. God made man to have one wife and enter into the covenant of holy matrimony whereby the two become one and a holy soul tie is established between the couple. When we choose to be intimate with people and have not entered into holy matrimony with them but are just involved casually, a soul tie is created that is unholy and it opens us up to attack by satan. If the one that we choose to be intimate with has been intimate with others, then we are opened up to receiving any demons which they may have collected along the way.

The fourth door of legal access for satan is opened when we participate in activities of the occult such as witchcraft, control and manipulation, divination and fortune telling, self-medication with alcohol and/or drugs (both legal and illegal street drugs), and going to the witch doctor. These activities open us to satan because we are seeking knowledge from the powers of darkness and not trusting Father God about our lives and our future.

If we opened any of these four doors of legal attack by satan unknowingly or even knowingly when we were in the world before we received Jesus into our lives, we need to close these doors, otherwise satan has legal access to continue to trip us up and harass us as we try to walk out our new lives with Jesus. Father God cares about our new lives in Christ and has shared this prayer that will close the four doors of legal harassment by satan:

Heavenly Father,

I thank you for your son, Jesus Christ of Nazareth, who went to the cross for me. He is my Lord and Savior!

Jesus, I reject the spirit of fear. I send it straight to the foot of the cross for Jesus Christ of Nazareth to deal with. I refuse to be angry. I reject anger and I send it straight to the foot of the cross for Jesus Christ of Nazareth to deal with. I refuse to participate in sexual promiscuity. I reject the spirit of lust and I send it straight to the foot of the cross for Jesus Christ of Nazareth to deal with. I will only be intimate with my legally wedded spouse or the members of the Godhead. I will not participate in activities of the occult. I reject witchcraft and control and manipulation and I will not seek out the future through divination. I will not go to the witch doctor or drink to excess. I send all of these activities of the occult and

54

witchcraft straight to the foot of the cross for Jesus Christ of Nazareth to deal with.

Jesus, I ask that you would close these four doors of legal attack and harassment by satan and seal them shut with your precious blood.

Jesus, I ask that you would sever any unholy or unhealthy soul ties that I may have established and send back to them what belongs to them and bring back to me what belongs to me washed in the precious blood of Jesus.

Jesus, I choose today to forgive anyone who may have ever hurt me, whether they knew it or not. I release them to you and I ask that you would bless them richly with every good gift you have given me and that they would come to know how deeply you love them.

Jesus, if there is any spirit in me that is not of you, I ask that you would take it away right now in Jesus Name. Lord, I ask that you would fill me to overflowing with your Holy Spirit and that every single part of my heart would be touched by your love and any parts of my mind that were hurt would also be touched by your oil of glory so that I would know that I am yours through and through, in Jesus name I pray. Amen.

Opening Our Hearts to Jesus

Jesus is the vine and He offers us all the opportunity to be grafted in to Him. His Father is the vine dresser and knows how to take care of us best. He knows which season we are in - whether we need fertilizing to encourage new growth, or whether we need pruning to strip away dead things which are simply taking away our strength. Jesus repeatedly told His disciples that He only did what He saw His Father doing. Jesus always looked to His Father for guidance and reflected His Father's heart well. Father God parted the heavens and declared "this is my beloved Son, in whom I am well pleased!" (Matthew 3:17)

By the time Jesus had fulfilled His destiny on earth, He reflected His Father so well that Mary, who had been one of His followers and disciples from early in His ministry, mistook Him for a gardener (John 20:14-16)! The more we look to Jesus and consider what He wants to bring forth in every situation, the more we will reflect Him and the more others (who may not yet know Him as we do) will see Him in us (1 Corinthians 13:12).

Letting God Touch you Directly

Jesus shared a final meal with His disciples, those whom He was teaching and who were close to Him. After He served them the wine which was His Blood and the Bread of life which was His Body (Matthew 26:26-28), the disciples were brought into union with Him and our tradition of Communion was established. Jesus then washed their feet (John 13:14-17) because He wanted to get the last remnants of the world off of them, to take away the dirt of the world from their lives so that they could walk cleanly into the fullness of their destinies through salvation once He went to the Cross and was no longer with them in person to guide them. He knew He had planted the seeds of Hope deep within their hearts and had consistently shown them to look to the Father for guidance as they made their way through the world, claiming new ground everywhere they went for the Kingdom of God.

When people pray for you and God touches you, be willing to allow Him to go low in your life to wash away the remnants of the world that may be trying to hold onto you, holding you back from walking freely into your destiny in the Lord. If your legs feel weak when others are praying for you and it becomes difficult to stand, let the Lord overwhelm you with His weightiness, the Kabod of His Glory, and be willing to go lower (to the floor) with God so that He can give you what you need through a direct encounter with Him and His Love. Let Him equip you with what He alone knows you need in order to walk out His plan for your destiny.

Jesus is and was the first fruits of many (1 Corinthians 15:23) and it is only because He laid His life down that we too can overcome this fallen world. Follow Jesus; follow His example for how to resist the enemy while sharing the Word of your testimony and because of the Power of the Blood of Jesus, you too shall overcome the constraints of your old life, that life that was still held in the grips of the world. Father God takes great delight in looking upon us as we are transformed more and more into the fullness of Christ. Once we choose to follow Jesus, we are "hidden in Christ" (Colossians 3:3). We are also seated with Christ in the Heavenlies (Ephesians 2:6) and have access to the very mind of Christ which equips us to overcome the world while also becoming the world's solution to all sorts of challenges which used to perplex us and defeat us. Because of Christ, we walk in victory - no longer merely being victims of the "storms" of the world. As we access the mind of Christ, renewing our minds, we cannot help being transformed! The Holy Spirit guides us in all truth (John 16:13) and convicts us (John 16:8) of areas where we need to receive and apply the Truth of the Word in our lives. For we shall "know the truth and the truth shall set us free" (John 8:32). As we grow in truth, we bear greater and greater testimony to the transformative power of Christ in our lives. When the Father looks upon us, He sees the effect that His Son, Jesus, our Lord and Savior, has had upon us and this surrender of our lives brings Glory to Jesus. Only Jesus could transform us so gloriously! His Love never fails (Psalm 136)! Truly, the Glory of the Lord is upon us and we shall do even greater things (John 14:12-14) when Jesus Himself is our starting place! As we grow in Christ, His Glory becomes ever more evident within our lives and eventually the entire earth will be covered with the Glory of the Lord (Habakkuk 2:14) as more and more brothers and sisters rise up and let their lights shine (Matthew 5:16). We were made to reflect Christ, the Light of the World (John 8:12), who came to shatter the darkness while undoing the works of evil as we walk in the authority Jesus alone gives us. It is time for us to rise and shine that the whole world will know that the Father so loved that He sent His only begotten Son (John 3:16) to be the first fruits of many (1 Corinthians 15:23).

How to "Walk it Out" as a Christian

Lots of people will tell you that you need to "walk it out" as a Christian, but you do not usually hear anyone teaching on how to do just that. "Walking it out" means that you live out Christianity as a lifestyle. Christianity should not just be a "Sunday morning moment." It is a lifestyle where you do all things "as unto the Lord" (Colossians 3:23). First you need to stop looking at your circumstances and set your sights on Jesus and then you can run your race. You need to invite Jesus into every area of your heart. If He is in Heaven making sure there is a mansion prepared for us (John 14:2), then the least we can do is make Him enough room in our hearts. If we invite Him in, He ought to be able to take over. Actually making Him the Lord of our life is where our Journey as a Christian really begins; it is only when Jesus is truly the Lord of our lives that we can begin to experience the transforming power Jesus alone gives us access to. It is only through Jesus that we can really enter in to living life and life more abundant (John 10:10).

Everything comes down to choice and free will. God has given man free will because God wants to know that we freely choose Him. So our choice while we are in the land of the living down here on Earth comes down to a choice between God's way or the world's way. Another way to look at it is that it comes down to a choice between the two trees that were first talked about back in the Garden of Eden - the tree of the fruit of the Knowledge of Good and Evil and the Tree of Life. Sometimes we need to step back from the situation and consider what it is that we think we are in need of? Are we trying to gain information or knowledge for knowledge's sake and if we are, we need to realize that this is actually choosing to eat from the Tree of the Knowledge of Good and Evil and that does not end well.

God's currency is faith. The Bible tells us on many different occasions that it is impossible to please God without faith. God wants to know that we trust Him, no matter what things look like around us. He wants to know that we have truly made His Son, Jesus Christ, the Lord of our life. He wants to know in every single situation that we choose God and His way over man, the world's way, and death. When we consider our choices in light of this information, it seems to make the choice a whole lot simpler: I would always choose life over death. I would always choose God's way over the world's way because I have seen the devastation that the world brings to people who are unsuspecting and do not know the spiritual war that they are caught up in. In addition to these things, I also know that God is a masterful mathematician and I know that when I invest in Him there is such an incredible multiplication in the fruit that is found afterwards that it is stunning. So I choose to follow Jesus. I choose to place my trust in God. I choose to invest my faith in His Supernatural Kingdom knowing that what He's bringing forth is far greater than anything I could ever even begin to imagine! (1 Corinthians 2:9)

The Transforming Power of the Word

We need to learn who it is that God says we are so that we can begin to become the sons of God and offer the same freedom in the spirit to others who have no hope yet. The whole earth groans for the revealing of the sons of God (Romans 8:19), those people who have chosen to allow God's holy Word to transform their lives and to yoke their minds to the mind of Christ so that they have the solutions that the earth is crying out for. We have a role to play in the redeeming of the entire earth and it is only as man rises up and walks in the authority that was originally given to him in the Garden of Eden that God's plan will begin to truly unfold. We have the opportunity to work with God as we bring the hope of Jesus to each broken heart we encounter along the way. We also have a responsibility to lead lives of integrity, demonstrating that our character has been transformed because we know Jesus. If any man says that he is of the kingdom, he ought to walk in a manner worthy of Jesus (1 John 2:6). The only way to do this is to learn how Jesus led His life, how He ministered to others, and how He says that we can live our lives as well. The kingdom of God does not come by observation alone (Luke 17:20).

You see sometimes that's the key question: are we actually willing to receive what Jesus has for us and act upon it? Christianity is not something that one can simply talk about. God wants us to experience Him and His great Love for us. He doesn't want us to just talk about how we believe He is. That's why the Bible tells us that *"they overcame by the Blood of the Lamb, the Word of their*

Testimony, and not loving their (ol59 d) lives unto death" (Revelation 12:11). We need to be willing to be changed by the Bible. We need to be willing to see what it is that the Holy Spirit is pointing out for us to address within our daily lives so that we can come into alignment with who God made us to be. The only way that we can do this is to actually work towards renewing our minds by reading what God says and refusing to continue to listen to what the world says! That is how we are transformed. However, it's something that we need to participate in. No one else can do it for us.

One of the most amazing gifts that Jesus gives each Christian Believer is the ability to actually finally become who it is that God made them to be. Over the course of my life there were different times when I was not happy with the person I had become, but I didn't have any idea of how to go about changing myself. The beauty of the gift of Jesus and God's Love Letter to us in the Holy Bible is that when we take the scriptures that describe how God made us to be and how He sees us, and we stand firm upon them, we can actually be transformed by them (Romans 12:2) into who it is that He made us to be all along. I call this "Scriptural Warfare" and I believe that it is one of the most effective tools that any Christian has for overcoming the character flaws that used to just completely overwhelm us and prevent us and block us from changing our ways.

One great example of using Scriptural Warfare was when I was trying to quit smoking cigarettes and my husband was still smoking two packs of cigarettes a day. The only way that I was able to overcome my desire to smoke was by launching scripture at the thought that I might want to smoke a cigarette. For example, when that thought would come, I would declare out loud: "I can do all things through Christ Jesus who strengthens me" (Philippians 4:13). Another thing I would do is: I would picture a cigarette and next to it I would picture Jesus and it was pretty clear who I would reach for.

Jesus says to "Follow" Him; I believe that He means for us to follow the example that He gave us within the pages of the Bible. We need to take a look at how He overcame the world and then use His ways so that we too can completely overcome the world and be transformed from Glory to Glory (2 Corinthians 3:18). One of the greatest ways to do this is to "mine (dig through) the Bible" for scriptures that will help us to stand firm upon His promises. Scriptures like: "Christ in me is the hope of glory" (Colossians 1:27) or "greater is He who is in me than he who is in the world" (1 John 4:4). When you find yourself being tempted by satan, declare scripture out loud as if you are launching a Scriptural Throwing Star or machete right at satan's forehead! Almost makes it fun...

After Jesus was water baptized, the Holy Spirit led Him into the wilderness to Fast. At this point in time, Jesus was growing closer and closer to Father God while worshipping Him in the wilderness. However, at this same time, satan was doing whatever it was that he could in order to tempt Jesus. So during 40 days of Fasting, Jesus was being tempted all along! He never gave in to the temptation!! At the end of His Fast when satan came back to tempt Him once again, He defeated satan by quoting scripture and reminding him, "it is written…" (Luke 4:4) each time satan tried to tempt Him. Even satan knows scripture and he knows that it's the Truth and he knows that the Truth is what will set us free (John 8:32). Only the Truth will set us free so we need to follow Jesus and use the resources that He's given us within the pages of the Holy Bible in order to fill up with Scriptural Weapons that we can throw right at satan when he tries to tempt us. Remember, the Bible tells us that when we are being tempted, God will always provide a way out (1 Corinthians 10:13). I believe that all we will ever need to make our way through the world is contained within the pages of the Bible and that as we live our lives led by the Holy Spirit, we will know the ultimate loving relationship with Father God through Jesus!

Making Jesus Christ the Lord of Your Life

For many, many years I was a "Believer" in name only. By this I mean that I believed God existed and I believed Jesus was real and that He did what they said He did in the Bible and I believed that the Holy Spirit existed. I had "head knowledge" of all of these things, but I had not had a specific experience with any of the members of the Godhead; I had no "heart connect" with the Godhead. I had not yet allowed Jesus to be the Lord of my Life and for that reason, there was no real change within my heart - I was still simply trying to make it through the world on my own, day by day. I was in "survival mode" - just trying to make it through another day by dealing with what life (or the world) threw my way. I was trying to "fit in" to the world, to be accepted and liked by man and only standing up for God when it was convenient. I thought everything was okay because I was not doing anything too bad, nothing worse than most people, as I tried to make my way through the world.

At one point in my life when I was feeling particularly low, I was reading a book and in it the woman had gone to the store to buy some things. As she came out of the store, three men grabbed her and asked for her money. One man had his arm across her neck and she could not breathe or get her money to give it to them. So she called on heaven. Heaven responded by sending a bright white light down which touched her and gave her the ability to fling the money out of her pocket. The man whose arm was across her throat let go of her and the other men took her money and ran. As soon as I read this, I said out loud: "I want to see that!" I had always felt that there was more to God than I had experienced.

Baptized By His Love

God answered my request the next day by sending His bright, white light down from heaven while I was at a stop light in my car. The beam of bright, white light came down from heaven, went through the roof of my car and entered the top of my head, filling me completely full with the pure, unconditional Agape Love of God. It was such an amazing experience that I said out loud: "If no one here on earth ever loves me again, it doesn't matter. God loves me"! The next thing that I said was: "If we could only bottle this, we would have no more war... until we ran out". The last thing I said was: "I really ought to ask my mother if she wants to come and live with me." It was a powerful experience; it changed my heart because I knew that the God who breathed the Universe into existence loved me and He was LOVE!

To be completely honest, I never told anyone about it at the time because I had never heard of anyone else having such an experience and I did not want anyone to try to talk me out of what I had experienced; I did not want man to ruin my beautiful moment with God. So I hugged that encounter with God close to my heart and knew that no matter what, God Loved me! This was the beginning of my heart connecting to God.

About eight years later, I met a man and all he talked about was Jesus. He told everyone he could about how Jesus was the only way to return to the Father. We got married and started our lives together as Christians. The problem was that although he talked about Jesus, he did not truly walk with Him. As I learned more and more about Jesus, I wanted more and more of Him in my life. I started going to every single meeting that I could where I would learn more about Jesus, Father God, and the Holy Spirit. I went out on the streets of the inner city to let others know that no matter what their lives were like and no matter how far away from God they felt they were, He was only one step away from them and He Loved them.

I was gone so much that my husband became convinced I was having an affair with another man even though I always asked him to come with me no matter where I was going. He kept accusing: "Who is he? What's his name? Who is this man"? I answered, "His name is Jesus and He says He misses you". Sadly, my husband chose to listen to the lies that satan was speaking about me and accused me of adultery.

Choosing Freedom Through Forgiveness

The good news is that I realized that with all of the struggles and challenges my husband had when trying to walk with Jesus, he must have a very important destiny with Jesus. I know that until everyone is in their proper position, the Body of Christ cannot move forward. So I prayed for my husband. I prayed for his heart to open that he could receive what Jesus had for him. I released forgiveness to my husband and released him to Jesus that he might receive what Jesus had for him. One day I was talking to God about how sad my heart was about all the things that I had been accused of by my husband, the one who was supposed to love me more than anyone else on earth. As I talked with God, I suddenly understood the power of what Jesus actually did for me on the cross. You see, up until that point I thought that since I wasn't there 2000 years ago and I did not raise my hand to vote to crucify Jesus, I could not be blamed for Him going to the Cross. I was willing to take the benefit of the Cross without looking at my role in Jesus going to the Cross.

When we talk about how Jesus took away the sin of the world, we are skipping over the true reality of what happened on the Cross. That day as I spoke with God, I realized that everything that had ever happened in my life that made me truly sad and hurt my heart, and every bad thing that I had ever done to other people as I committed sins, and every moment that I had lived my life without Jesus (sin of omission), Jesus experienced on the cross. He lived my life as if He was me having these things done to Him and as if He was being falsely accused by satan of doing those things to me. I believe that Jesus experienced each person's life while hanging on the cross - each person who has ever lived, each person who is alive right now, and each one who will ever live. As Jesus lived our lives on the cross, He also experienced the position of our hearts and He knew us intimately and that is how He was able to say: "Forgive them. They know not what they do." This is also why Jesus is able to lift our head and call us friend, because He has lived our lives and has intimate knowledge of our hearts. The Bible says: "No greater gift than a man lay down his life for that of another." (John 15:13)

We cannot choose to just receive the Blessing of the Cross while refusing to consider the cost of what Jesus suffered just for us while upon the Cross. He paid the price for each of us while upon the Cross. The question is - what will we do with the new start in life that Jesus gives us? Will we give Him what He paid for? Will we give Him our lives as we make Him the Lord of our lives and begin to live for Him and His Kingdom? Will we allow Jesus to begin to change our hearts so that we can become who it is that Father God truly made us to be? Will we allow ourselves to be changed by the Word of God? The Bible says that when Jesus came to earth, the "Word became flesh." We have an amazing opportunity with this new life that Jesus has given us – we can allow ourselves to also become the Word of Life by getting as much of the Word of God into us as possible. When we make Jesus Christ the Lord of our lives, we can step into life and life more abundant as we allow Him to transform us and we begin to become Love.

When Jesus completed His assignment on the cross, satan knew that all was lost; satan knew he no longer had any true authority. Father God gave authority over all things on earth and in heaven to Jesus (Matthew 28:18). Jesus in turn gave man authority: "If you ask me anything in my name, I will do it (John 14:14)." The only way satan can accomplish his plans is through "stealing" our authority by fooling us into believing he has power.

When we are born again, our Spirit Man is completely reborn and is extremely sensitive to the Spiritual Realm. satan is well aware of this and he also knows that as young, baby Christians we're not fully confident in our identity in Christ. So satan will cause one of his minions to whisper thoughts near us and when we pick up on those thoughts it is possible for us to be fooled into thinking that they are our own thoughts. The minute we do that, we have come into agreement with those thoughts and then they do become ours. The same is true with lying symptoms and sickness. Sometimes we will experience the emotions of someone else and think that they are ours and in doing so, we take ownership of it and then it is ours. The scripture "If any man be in Christ, he is a new creation, all things are made new (2 Corinthians 5:17)" offers an incredible promise from Father God! We can use that promise to refuse to receive the spirit of infirmity as well as to refuse to continue to be the way we were before we made Jesus Christ the Lord of our lives. The challenge is that satan knows that we are not yet fully confident so he will continue asking us over and over again, "did He really say that? Did He really say that? Are you sure that what He said is enough? Are you sure that what Jesus did on the Cross was enough to cover you and the terrible things you did? Are you sure? Are you sure?" Yes! I am sure! I have no doubt that God is good. I have no doubt that God is the giver of all good gifts and I have no doubt that what Jesus accomplished on the Cross is good enough for me. I also have no doubt that His love never fails!

Receiving What Jesus Offers

The Kingdom of Heaven is like a field in which a man found a treasure of such great value that he went home and he sold everything he had in order to buy the entire field (Matthew 13:44). You are that treasure in that field. The Lord purchased you through the precious blood of His Son, Jesus Christ, who is our Lord and savior.

The Kingdom of Heaven is also like a field in which a man planted a good crop. The good crop is the word that God has placed in your heart and that word is there to bear much fruit. However, the enemy comes along in the night to sow his tares (Matthew 13:24-29), his weeds, and even his lying symptoms.

When Jesus received the Holy Spirit, the Holy Spirit then led Him out into the Wilderness where He could choose to grow closer to God. Satan tried to tempt Jesus as He fasted and prayed and worshipped. I believe that if satan has sown a lying symptom into your field, he's trying to tempt you into coming into agreement with the lying symptom. Once you agree with that symptom and tell others that you "have" whatever the particular affliction is, you will have partnered with and received that spirit of infirmity. The key is for you to absolutely refuse to receive that lying symptom! Yes, there are facts, but we know

Jesus and He is the Truth! He is the beginning and the end and He gets the final word! Do whatever you can to not give in to the temptation to tell other people about this word curse that satan is trying to put upon you. Instead, declare to others that even though science might think that this is the case, you know the truth and the truth is that Jesus Christ will set you free of any spirit of infirmity or spirit of affliction and anything else sent by the enemy to undermine the life more abundant that Jesus Christ has for you. The key is to not come into agreement with satan by telling people you "have" it...that is taking ownership of it!

Know that we are praying with you in agreement that satan would be shown to be the liar that he is and that the Truth would come out and the truth is that you belong to Jesus - He purchased you and it is by His stripes that you are healed!

In the mighty name of Jesus, I break off all word curses, and I release the truth which is that Jesus Christ is our Lord and Savior and that the Holy Spirit lives within us and that where the Spirit of the Lord is there is liberty and freedom and there is no room for disease. Thank you Jesus, for the life which you are breathing into us right now. It is in your Holy, precious name that I pray, Amen.

The Power of Our Words

Lately, the Lord has really been impressing upon me the vital importance of what it is that I come into agreement with through my words. The power of life and death is within the tongue (Proverbs 18:21) and a man does not enter into building something without counting the cost (Luke 14:28) so I need to learn to count the cost of what my words are going to be partnering with before I speak them. I need to consider whether my words are going to build up or tear down. When building something, it's important to measure twice and cut once. The Bible tells us that we're going to be accountable for every idle word (Matthew 12:36) and an idle word is a word that's not working. It can also be our words when we talk more about worldly things rather than talking about the things of the Lord and what He has done within our lives.

In general, our circumstances separate into three categories that I've noticed. The first category would be circumstances that are actually the consequence of a less than good choice on our part. The second set of circumstances would be an opportunity for us to develop a greater level of Integrity within our moral character. The third set of circumstances would be an opportunity for us to allow the Lord to lead us through what would seem to be a valley in our lives. In this case, it is only when we allow the Lord to bring us out of our circumstances that we are then able to gain a whole new level of authority over that particular issue within our lives. Remember, the Bible tells us that *"they overcame by the blood of the Lamb, the word of their testimony, and not loving their (old) lives unto death"* (Revelation 12:11). I believe that what Jesus accomplished on the cross and his presence in my life have led me to the point where I no longer want to hold on to my old way of living life and when I let go and give it to Him, He will bring me through. I believe that when I share the testimony of what Jesus did for me, it gives the next person hope and Jesus is able to redeem my past experience while at the same time lead another person through that same valley of difficulty. What an awesome God we serve!

I believe that our circumstances offer us the opportunity to increase our trust in God. I believe He is always reaching out to us, asking: "do you trust me on this?" The Bible tells us that He turns all things together for the good of those who love Him and are called according to His purposes (Romans 8:28). The Bible also tells us that He chose us out of the world before the foundation of the world (Ephesians 1:4). That's amazing! I believe that God is always wanting to increase our faith. The Bible tells us that Jesus is the author and perfecter of our faith (Hebrews 12:2). I believe that we are continuously being afforded opportunities to choose to trust God and invest our faith in Him and that when we do, we receive a Kingdom reward. Anytime that we invest our faith in the Kingdom there is an amazing Harvest to be yielded, treasure in heaven as it were! God is the god of increase and as we choose to place our faith in Him, He is a rewarder of that faith. It is impossible to please God without faith (Hebrews 11:6). Every time we place faith in God, we please Him. What an awesome thing, to be able to please the Creator of the Universe, the one True Living God!

Being Transformed

As long as we simply continue on as we always have, just living our lives and minding our own business, the enemy is succeeding. Sure, we will eventually go to Heaven someday, but is that really fulfilling God's plan for us or the kingdom? What about being transformed from glory to glory (2 Corinthians 3:18)? Did you notice that our starting place is glory? God never intended for us to simply survive, one day miraculously actually making it to Heaven. The Kingdom is NOT a physical destination; it is a way of living life by truly entering into life more abundant (John 10:10). Today! What about choosing to be transformed by the renewing of our minds (Romans 12:2)? Simple, but not always easy, for satan will always question our faith every step of the way. "Did He really say that?" Or "who do you think you are? Don't you remember how you totally blew it way back when...?"

In short, anything negative or past tense is the voice of the enemy trying to re-establish prominence in our heads. The real battleground is in our thought life and that is why the Bible tells us to *take every thought captive to the obedience of the Lordship of Jesus Christ."* (2 Corinthians 10:5) Have you been forgiven by what Jesus paid for you on the cross and have you forgiven yourself? Jesus paid dearly for ALL of you - mind, soul, spirit and body. It's time to actually submit to the Lordship of Jesus in our lives and let Him heal our broken areas - He is the master physician and He already knows exactly what you need. He has a plan and it truly is a glorious one. Receive it! If there is a temptation you are experiencing or an old bad habit you've been convicted of by the Holy Spirit, let Jesus lead you to freedom. He says: "follow me" and He gives great examples of how we can follow Him straight into a life of overcoming the world. The most effective way of defeating the enemy's attempts to derail our Christian walk through sending temptation our way is by releasing scripture over our lives. For example, *"I can do all things through Christ Jesus who strengthens me"* or *"greater is He who is in me* (Jesus in my heart) *than he who is in the world* (satan tempting me)". God's Word never goes forth without accomplishing that for which it was intended (Isaiah 55:11).

The Power of our Testimony

The Bible tells us that they overcame by the Blood of the Lamb, the Word of their Testimony and not loving their lives unto death (Revelation 12:11). What does that mean? It means that because Jesus overcame the world and we are His, we have everything we need in order to overcome the world. The Bible tells us that in Him we've been given every divine thing that we need in order to succeed (2 Peter 1:3). We've been given access to the mind of Christ, therefore we have the solutions of Heaven! Jesus tells us that because the world hated Him and we are no longer of this world once we belong to Him, the world is going to hate us too (John 15:18-19). We need to just get over it. We need to actually look on the world hating us as a great blessing because it lets us know that we are on the right track. We are headed towards Victory! Jesus overcame everything and then gave that Victory to us in John 17; if only we would walk in Victory, knowing that we are His. After all, we get to read the end of the book and we **know** how it ends. We know we've been given everything we need in Jesus and therefore we are overcomers also. The question then becomes, what is the Word of Our Testimony? What is the evidence of Jesus in our lives? What is changing in our lives that we ourselves could not change on our own? How can we demonstrate to the world the ultimate importance of having Jesus in our lives? What is it that Father God wants to show the world through our lives? I believe Father God wants to show the world His plan to help us all become who it is He always made us to be and who it is that He's had faith that we would become. Even when the world gives up on us, Father God never does! Probably because His Son, Jesus, paid such a high price for our success!

Once we reconcile ourselves to the fact that the world is not going to like us, then we are able to move on to some of the greatest opportunities ever! We are able to allow Father God to use us to open the eyes of the blind. We're able to allow Father God to use us, those thought of as foolish, to confound those who think themselves to be wise. Over the course of the past year, Father God has been opening my eyes more and more to understanding that statement on a whole new level. I'm now understanding that He is using the foolish me (who I know I am today) and who I now know has little understanding of Kingdom ways or the thoughts of God, to confound my wise self, as I always thought I had things pretty much figured out! Only Father God has a sense of humor like that! I love His humor, don't you? All of Heaven echoes with the rumblings of the laughter coming forth from the Throne Room! The bottom line is, I figure if I can get God to have a good laugh then I'm doing something right. In reality though, I believe Him when He tells me in the Bible that He rejoices over me. I don't need to earn His rejoicing over me - that's just who He is!

Choosing Unity

The worldly way is to always classify things, to identify things and put them into little categories so that we can better understand them while Heaven's way is to embrace things. Heaven is not about division, rather Heaven is about unity and walking in unison, embracing the fullness of the spectrum. As Christians, we have gone to great lengths to establish differences in Doctrine that are then turned into the foundational points for creating different Denominations. This is not creation, rather it is simply division. God is not about division. Rather, He is the God of multiplication. God is about Jesus, and Jesus included everyone when He said "Forgive them they know not what they do." I believe that the time has come for us to focus on what it is that unifies us, and that should be Jesus. In short, I believe every single Denomination has become a point of sadness within God's heart. I believe that is time for us to let go of our differences and instead grab hands with the person next to us so that we can run together in unison, following Jesus! On a personal note, I love words and I love plays on words. And when I take apart the word "Denomination", it comes to mean: out from the name. So I believe that as we construct all these different Denominations, we are actually removing ourselves farther and farther out from and away from the Name of Jesus. Jesus was never about division, in fact He emphatically illustrated that concept to His disciples with the statement: "If they're not against us then they're with us (Mark 9:38). It is time to embrace the victory that Jesus won for us already and enforce it by tearing down all those things that keep us separated and focus on coming into unity, following Christ who is the head so that we can walk together as a functioning body, a body worthy of Christ's sacrifice on our behalf. Let's share hope with others as we share our testimonies of what Jesus has done in our lives with others, introducing them to the importance of Jesus and the Bible today.

The Coming Harvest

We need to continuously be interceding for those who don't yet know the Lord. We need to ask Jesus to go into the heart of the enemy camp and reveal His heart to people who have been ensnared by satan's shame tactics. We also need to ask God to reveal the Truth to people whom satan has appeared to disguised as an angel of light (2 Corinthians 11:14) so that they would know the truth and the truth would set them free (John 8:32). We are at a critical time in the History of Christianity. We are on the eve of the greatest Harvest ever and we are poised on the very edge of the greatest outpouring of Father God's Spirit! However, before we can successfully bring in the Lord's Harvest, we need laborers (Luke 10:2). We need to partner with the Lord and take those He sends to us "under our wing" to disciple them. We will need trained, healed and equipped laborers to disciple the upcoming Harvest. There will be more than enough work to go around so we needn't worry about losing our "Position" to someone else. Let's just submit to His Lordship and partner with Him to disciple the Laborers He is bringing into His Kingdom to help us with the Harvest. After all...He is LORD of the Harvest!

The Lord's Ways are higher than our Ways (Isaiah 55:9). He is doing a new thing! *"No eye has seen, nor ear heard, nor the heart of man imagined what it is that The Lord is preparing for those that Love Him."* (1 Corinthians 2:9) He told us to pray for Him to bring the laborers *"for the harvest is ripe but the workers are few."* (Luke 10:2 and Matthew 9:37) He warns us over and over to not judge others for as we *"measure so shall we be measured."* (Matthew 7:2) He warns us that we cannot see others as we should because when we go after the speck in someone else's eye, we really should look to the plank in our own eye (Matthew 7:5) because it blocks our ability to see others as we should.

He tells us we need to *"grow in grace"* (2 Peter 3:18) for freely we received His grace and we should freely give (Matthew 10:18) it to others. He tells us that only He knows the condition of the heart of another (Romans 2:2). How many people have we hurt by judging them based on their appearance alone? What if we prayed for The Lord of the Harvest to send the workers and He sent them only to have us refuse to receive them because they did not look like we thought they should? What if instead of offering grace and looking for His treasure in their hearts and encouraging them to become who He made them to be, we met them with hard-hearted judgment? What have we done with the talents He has given us - Have we invested hope in others, knowing that His grace is sufficient? If we chose to embrace them with grace, might it just be that He could touch them and work a "miracle" in them just as He did in us? What if He has been answering our prayer to send the laborers all along, but we have missed it because we have been preoccupied with our own thoughts on how the laborers should look and as we judged them and dismissed them as having no value to us as they were, we too may be found to be lacking on judgment day. What have we invested in others?

Have we spent our talents on teaching others of His never ending Love? Are we going to act like the elder brother when the prodigal brother comes home (Luke 15:11-32)? The elder brother had been with the Father all along, yet did not understand the compassionate Love of the Father; he was not willing to invest his inheritance in celebrating the return of his brother who had slipped away. What if it is only someone who has been judged and found wanting by man yet knows they are completely loved by the Father that is able to minister to the people whom The Lord is drawing into His heart at this time? We need to ask The Lord to search our hearts for any tares that have grown amongst the seeds He has planted in our hearts. (Matthew Chapter 13)

Loving Your Neighbor as Yourself

As "Saved" Christians under the influence of the Spirit of Religion, we thought we came first in His affection, however, He tells us that "the first shall come last and the last shall come first" (Matthew 20:16). What if He has even more compassion and love for those who have been hurt by "Saved Believers" who claim they are doing His work? He promises a significant return on what people suffer on His behalf – what is the cost of one's dignity and worth? He promises the same reward (wage) to ALL those working in His vineyard, regardless of when they begin to work for Him (Matthew Chapter 20). We need to feed all we meet with His Bread of Life and offer them a drink of His living water for we never know when we may be entertaining one of the Lord's own angels (Hebrews 13:2). We have been given all we need in His Son, Jesus, (2 Peter 1:3) and the Holy Spirit is the down payment on our inheritance as sons and daughters of Father God (Ephesians 1:14). What are we choosing to spend/invest our inheritance (talents) on?

The astounding promise of God is that: *No eye has seen, nor ear heard, nor the heart of man imagined what it is that God has prepared for those who love Him* (1 Corinthians 2:9). We need to remember to keep our eyes on Jesus just as He always kept His eyes on the Father to see what He was doing and what He saw. For it is *"the glory of God to conceal a matter, but the glory of kings is to search out a matter"* and the Kingdom of God is like a man who finds a treasure within a field and he hides it and then for *"joy over it he goes and sells all that he has and buys that field"* (Matthew 13:44). Father God sent His precious Son to buy back (or redeem) the world and all the treasures (his children) that were stuck in the world. As His sons and daughters, we are destined to rule and reign with Him as a Royal Priesthood, and as such we need to be looking for those who are still stuck in the world so that we can call out the treasure within them *"for we have this treasure in earthen vessels"* (2 Corinthians 4:7).

Discipling Leaders for The Lord's Harvest

I believe that we are still in the final stages of preparing for the Billion Soul Harvest. For years we have been praying in the laborers to help with this Harvest, and I believe that this is the time for us to go to the Highways and Byways to search out the ones He highlights to us. They need to be set free from where they have been stuck so that they can begin to be transformed by the renewing of their minds. We need to begin training and equipping them (also known as discipling them) to present the fullness of Jesus to the ones who will be coming in as the Lord's Harvest comes forth. We need to remember that Jesus paid the price to redeem everyone over two thousand years ago. It is our privilege to share the Good News with those who have not yet heard about or received what He did for them. We need to share it in a way that draws them to Him. What better way than by sharing our Joy of the Lord with them as we encourage them? We can let them know that no matter what their circumstances are or how far they feel they are away from Him, He is right there. He is always simply waiting for them to turn and see Him, waiting with His arms wide open to receive them. Once they receive Him and invite Him into their hearts, they have a clean slate. They are born again and **all** things are made new. It is then that the masterpiece of their lives can begin to come forth from the hand of the Master. We need to always remember to keep our eyes on Jesus and what it is that the Lord wants to do within each situation. It is never about circumstances, those are in reality distractions from the enemy, merely designed to draw our focus from the Father and His Kingdom. Instead, we should be continuously asking Him how we can partner with Him to bring His Kingdom forth, asking Him to see things through His eyes and with His heart.

Be Willing to be Poured Out

A Final Point to Ponder:

The first miracle attributed to Jesus was at the Wedding at Cana where they had run out of wine and His mother, Mary, told Him about it (John 2). Jesus told her that it wasn't His time yet, and Mary simply told the servants to do whatever Jesus told them to do. Jesus then told the servants to fill the six stone water pots to the brim with water and to then pour out some of it to take to the master of the feast. When the master of the feast tasted "the water that was made wine," he was amazed by the quality of it. Notice that Jesus never touched the water or spoke to it, He only told the servants at the wedding to use the six stone water purification pots by filling them to the brim. Throughout the Bible, Jesus tells us that He only ever does what He sees the Father do. I believe that when Mary first spoke to Him, He saw it was not time for Him to do anything, but when Mary exercised extreme faith by telling the servants *"whatever He says to you, do it,"* the very heart of God was moved and the first miracle occurred. Six (the number of water pots) is the number which points to man in the Bible and we as men are called to be "living stones" with which He can build His Spiritual house (1 Peter 2:5).

What if Jesus wants to fill us full of His Living Water and use us as living, stone vessels to turn that water into the new wine that He can pour out as He invites others in to His Kingdom Wedding Feast?

References

References are taken from the Bible (NKJV, KJV, NIV, ESV, The Passion Translation)

References of Hebrew and Greek are taken from the KJV Strong's Concordance

References are taken from "Unleashed and Ready to Empower" written by Trina Olson copyright 2019

References are taken from "1° Twist: Recalibrating Your Kingdom Compass" written by Edith Houghton copyright 2019

Cover Design by Edith Houghton and Trina Olson

 *Trina Olson was transformed in a moment when God pulled her car off an embankment while she was committing suicide. Since that time God has taken Trina on an incredible journey, revealing her true identity to her. God has impressed upon her heart a call to help others encounter Jesus to be empowered to become who it is that God has made them to be. She founded Radical Launch International Ministries in 2012 after graduating from the Global School of Supernatural Ministry.*

Edith Houghton gave her heart to Jesus at an early age only to then become caught up in the world. She served as an officer in the United States Navy where she quickly learned the value of teamwork and the importance of living a life of integrity. Upon re-dedicating her life to the Lord and giving him Lordship over her life, Edith's heart was ignited with a passion for the things of God and she attended many of the Christian conferences at the Global School of Supernatural Ministry under Randy Clark.

Trina and Edith have been traveling as itinerant ministers under Radical Launch for the past several years within the United States and overseas. This manual came about in response to the apparent need they observed over the course of their travels. Part of the Great Commission is for us as Christians to disciple nations and that is the hope behind this Radical Christianity 101: Empowering Your Disciples manual.

Unleashed Publishing, Inc

Unleashing the potential authors, editors, and illustrators of a generation.

CPSIA information can be obtained
at www.ICGtesting.com
Printed in the USA
JSHW031146070522
25625JS00002B/102